Get Slim
healthy and beautiful
and Fit

HOW TO ACHIEVE YOUR GOAL

We all want to be slim and healthy. And we all know that traditional diets are no help. Actually, all you need to reach this goal is a carefully chosen eating plan. Also, make sure you get enough exercise and don't overtax your body with too much alcohol, tobacco, or other toxins. On the following pages you'll find the eating plan you're looking for, featuring simple, flavorful recipes that are packed full of vitamins. Now that you're getting your daily supply of vitamins from your food, you can say goodbye to supplements.

NATURE'S MIRACLES

We cannot see vitamins, and yet we cannot survive without them. To thrive, our bodies need a certain amount of vitamins every day. These tiny little miracles provide no calories, but they function as our body's "laborers." Vitamins are involved in every metabolic process, are essential for the reproduction of cells, and strengthen our immune systems. In short: vitamins keep us healthy and happy. If we don't get enough of them, we soon start to feel weak and fall ill.

MINIATURE IMMIGRANTS

Vitamins are divided into two groups: fat-soluble vitamins (A, D, E, and K) and the water-soluble ones, the best known of which is vitamin C. Our bodies cannot make the most important vitamins; rather, we rely on a regular supply from the foods they eat. If we have the full requirement of a particular vitamin, the reserves will last between two weeks and two years, depending on the vitamin in question. Whether a vitamin is fat- or water-soluble determines just how long the reserves last.

VARIETY—THE SECRET TO WELL-BEING

We have just read how important these invisible miracles are. So how do we make sure to get enough of them without popping a bunch of pills? Easy: enjoy a wide variety of foods. Fruits and vegetables, whole-grain breads and cereals, milk and other dairy products provide a large amount of vitamins. However, traditional diets that contain only a few different foods are unlikely to provide all of the vitamins required. Also, think about your lifestyle. Smokers, for instance, require extra vitamins, as do expectant and nursing mothers, athletes, and those with compromised immune systems.

DAILY VITAMIN REQUIREMENTS IN FOOD

VITAMIN	FOOD
A	2 oz carrots or 12 oz apricots
D	9 oz mushrooms or $7^1/_2$ oz redfish
E	7 oz salsify or $^3/_4$ oz sunflower oil
K	3 oz broccoli or $^3/_4$ oz spinach
B_1	14 oz peas or 4 oz lean pork chop
B_2	1 lb salmon or $1^3/_4$ lb broccoli
B_6	6 oz salmon or $1^3/_4$ lb green beans
B_{12}	2 oz beef or 7 oz yogurt
Niacin	$6^1/_2$ oz oyster mushrooms or 5 oz liver
Folic acid	7 oz spinach or $5^1/_2$ oz Brussels sprouts
Pantothenic acid	10 oz mushrooms or $13^1/_2$ oz watermelon
Biotin	$3^1/_2$ oz green beans or 3 oz fennel
C	2 oz bell pepper or 5 oz orange

In order to stay fit and healthy, try to obtain your daily requirement of vitamins and minerals from the things you eat and drink (see chart above).

Slim Down

how to choose them, what to do

with Vitamins

GET SLIM AND STAY SLIM

• Do not make the supermodels your role models, it will only lead to frustration.

• Eat lots of fresh fruit and vegetables–there's no need to count the calories in these.

• Be a miser with fat. Use nonstick pans when sautéing, and grill fish, poultry, and meat.

• Choose low-fat fish, poultry, and meats. Watch the fat and calorie content in dairy products, such as milk, yogurt, and cheese.

• Avoid hidden fats in ready-made meals, take-out foods, baked goods, and other sweet treats.

• Don't weigh yourself every day. Your weight fluctuates daily, sometimes quite dramatically. Don't panic if your weight suddenly increases for no apparent reason.

• Don't forget the calories present in some popular beverages. Avoid lemonade, sodas, and other sweet fizzy drinks–they contain high amounts of sugar, and nothing that is good for you. Ideally, quench your thirst with fruit and vegetable juices. If you don't want to make your own, buy cartons of pure juice, which contains no water. If the bottle or carton is labeled "Nectar" or "Fruit Drink," it contains a lot of water and sugar.

TREAT VITAMINS WITH CARE

Vitamins need to be treated with a little TLC. Light, air, and heat will destroy them, so the following rules should be observed–especially in the case of fruit and vegetables:

* use as soon as possible
* if you need to store them, keep them in a cool and dark place
* do not peel or chop fruits or vegetables until just before cooking and/or eating
* wash as quickly as possible
* wash first, then chop or slice so that water-soluble vitamins do not leach out
* cook fruit and vegetables as little as possible; in order to retain the most vitamins, eat fruit and vegetables raw
* steam fruit and vegetables under a tightly fitting lid, in their own juices, or in just a tiny amount of liquid
* serve as soon as possible

Even just for preserving vitamins, it is worth investing in a steamer, or a steamer insert for a saucepan. Use only a small amount of water. Place the vegetables in the steamer insert, place the insert in the saucepan, cover with a lid, and steam over medium heat until just tender-crisp.

WHAT DESTROYS VITAMINS?

VITAMIN	MAIN ENEMIES
A	light, air
D	reasonably resilient vitamin
E	light, air, heat
K	reasonably resilient vitamin
B_1	heat, water
B_2	light, water
B_6	heat, water, cold
B_{12}	light, air, water
Niacin	water
Folic acid	light, heat, water (very sensitive)
Pantothenic acid	heat, water, acid,
Biotin	water
C	light, air, heat water

IMPORTANT: Do not leave newly bought fruit and vegetables unwrapped or at room temperature for longer than absolutely necessary. Use organic produce whenever possible.

Vitamins for Better Health

Vitamin	Good Sources
A	Green-leafed vegetables, yellow and red fruits and vegetables, eggs, butter, liver
D	Liver, meat, milk, fish, eggs, mushrooms
E	Vegetable fats (especially wheat germ and sunflower oils), cabbage, bell peppers, spinach, salsify, avocados, cereals/grains, nuts
K	Green vegetables, whole-grain breads and cereals, milk, meat
B_1	Sprouts, whole-grain breads and cereals, potatoes, sunflower seeds, egg yolks, pork, yeast
B_2	Sprouts, milk, whole-grain breads and cereals, meat, fish
B_6	Cabbage, leeks, bell peppers, soybeans, bananas, whole-grain breads and cereals, potatoes, nuts, meat, fish
B_{12}	Meat, vegetables containing lactic acid, milk, sour milk products, eggs, fish
Niacin	Potatoes, mushrooms, peas, whole-grain breads and cereals, meats, fish
Folic acid	Spinach, asparagus, fennel, beets, potatoes, orange juice, whole-grain breads and cereals, milk
Pantothenic acid	Broccoli, mushrooms, melons, egg yolks, whole-grain breads and cereals, yeast, liver, meat, milk, mushrooms
Biotin	Carrots, peas, sprouts, spinach, tofu, eggs, yeast, nuts, oats, milk, whole-grain breads and cereals, mushrooms
C	Citrus fruits, berries, kiwi, bell peppers, cabbage, spinach, potatoes

NEEDED FOR	SIGNS OF A DEFICIENCY	VITAMIN
Eye, skin, and hair health; cell protection; disease resistance; protection against cancer	Poor night vision; flaky skin; poor resistance to infection	A
Bone and skin health	Growth problems; decalcification of bones	D
Cell protection; liver detoxification; protection against cancer and heart disease (antioxidant)	Anemia; paleness; muscular weakness	E
Blood coagulation	Slow coagulation of blood	K
Release of energy from carbohydrates; combating stress; heart and muscle health; memory	Tiredness; loss of appetite; muscular, circulatory, and coronary weakness; cramps; poor performance	B_1
Converting proteins, fats and carbohydrates into energy; growth; disease resistance	Cracks on lips and at corners of mouth; dry skin; poor vitality	B_2
Protein metabolism; growth; skin, hair and nerve health; reproduction of blood cells	Tiredness; anemia; skin changes; loss of appetite	B_6
Cell construction and protection; disease resistance; reproduction of blood cells and tissues; growth	Anemia; tiredness; poor resistance to infections	B_{12}
Energy release in tissues and cells; skin, heart, and nerve health; growth	Nausea; diarrhea; depression	Niacin
Growth and reproduction of cells, particularly red blood cells; protection against heart attacks	Anemia; tiredness; poor resistance to infections	Folic acid
Releasing energy from foods; bones, skin, and hair health; hormone creation	Skin damage; dull hair; nervousness; poor resistance to infections	Pantothen-ic acid
Metabolism of carbohydrates, proteins, and fats; blood, nerve, skin, and hair health	Lethargy; loss of appetite; loss of hair; skin changes	Biotin
Immune system health; iron absorption; reproduction of blood cells; cell construction	Poor resistance to infection; lethargy; slow-healing wounds; growth problems; poor performance	C

Power
highly nutritious low-calorie meals
Week

GET SLIM & BE FIT

Are you feeling listless, weak, and tired? Would you like to lose a few pounds? Follow the menu suggestions given in our "Power Week" for just seven days, and you won't have to wait long to see the results!

THE PLAN

Following are meal suggestions for each day of the week, which you can follow as given or switch around to suit your whim. For the best start to your day, make a delicious breakfast of whole-grain flakes or coarsely ground cereal, fresh fruit, and low-fat yogurt after your shower. Those of us with a sweet tooth can add a tiny bit of honey or maple syrup. Or, spread some low-fat cottage cheese on a slice of whole-grain bread. Eat as much fresh fruit and vegetables as you like between meals. Quench your thirst with fruit and herbal teas, and mineral water with fruit juice for extra flavor and vitamins.

FOR BUSY PEOPLE

If you are unable to prepare two meals a day, choose a recipe and prepare it in the evening to eat the next day. Bring fresh fruit and low-fat, low-sugar yogurt for your lunch break. You can also take instant broth granules and add boiling water for a warming soup. Soothe any between-meal hunger pangs with an apple, some raw vegetables, or an occasional whole-grain roll.

THE WEEK'S MEALS

Monday

* Muesli with fresh fruit, or whole-grain bread
* Vegetable and Herb Salad, whole-grain roll
* Spanish Potato Tortilla ● Date and Pineapple Salad

Tuesday

* Blueberry and Banana Milk, whole-grain bread
* Curried Ginger Vegetables, brown rice
* Cauliflower and Broccoli Salad

Wednesday

* Muesli with fresh fruit, or whole-grain bread
* Indonesian Vegetable Soup ● Iced Pineapple and Almond Shake
* Fruited Raw Carrots ● Stovetop Spelt Cakes with Radishes

Thursday

* Raspberry and Strawberry Shake, whole-grain bread
* Spinach Salad with Oranges, whole-grain baguette
* Turnip and Turkey Fricassee, brown rice

Friday

* Muesli with fresh fruit, or whole-grain bread
* Stir-Fried Thai Vegetables, rice noodles
* Zucchini and Tomato Salad, rye baguette ● Jellied Fruit Tea with Grapes

Saturday

* Carrot and Tomato Yogurt, whole-grain bread
* Vegetable and Sprout Salad, whole-grain bread or roll
* Linguine with Raw Tomato Sauce ● Citrus Fruit Platter

Sunday

* fruit salad, whole-grain roll, low-fat cheese, and an egg
* Asparagus Salad ● Strawberry and Kiwi Salad
* Light Minestrone, whole-grain bread or roll

Spinach

and toasted

Salad with

pine nuts

Oranges

Serves 2: **2 oranges • 4 oz fresh spinach • 1 small red onion • 1-2 tbs red wine vinegar • Salt to taste • Black pepper to taste • 3 tbs olive oil • 1 tbs pine nuts (toasted)**

Peel the oranges and cut into segments. Wash and pick over the spinach, discarding any coarse stalks. Peel and halve the onion and slice thinly.

In a salad bowl, combine the vinegar, salt, pepper, and oil. Stir the oranges, spinach, and onion into the dressing. Sprinkle with the toasted pine nuts.

power

PER PORTION: 195 calories • 3 g protein • 14 g fat • 16 g carbohydrates

Vegetable and
with cashew nuts and fresh ginger
Sprout Salad

Roughly chop the cashew nuts and toast them in a dry nonstick pan until golden. Remove from the pan and set aside.

Serves 2:
2 tbs cashew nuts
Thumb-sized piece fresh ginger
1 small shallot
2 tbs sherry vinegar
Salt to taste
White pepper to taste
3 tbs sunflower oil
1 tbs sesame oil
1 small carrot
1 radish
2 oz cucumber
4 oz mixed sprouts

Peel and finely chop the ginger and shallots. Combine both with the vinegar, salt, and pepper, then add the two oils, and beat well.

Trim and peel the carrot, radish, and cucumber and grate coarsely. Rinse the sprouts in a sieve, drain well, and tear into bite-sized pieces. Combine with the grated vegetables, mix with the dressing, and arrange on two plates. Sprinkle with the toasted cashew nuts and serve immediately.

Sprouts

Set up your own little sprout farm on the windowsill so you have a constant supply of fresh vitamins. Fresh sprouts are full of beta carotene, vitamins E and K, and various B complex vitamins–including the rare B_{12}.

power

PER PORTION:
244 calories
4 g protein
22 g fat
9 g carbohydrates

Cauliflower and
Broccoli Salad

with creamy nutmeg sauce

Toast the almonds in a dry skillet until brown, then remove. Trim and wash the cauliflower and broccoli and cut into bite-sized florets. Peel and chop the broccoli stalks. Place the vegetables in a steamer insert.

Bring the stock to a boil in a saucepan. Place the steamer insert inside, cover tightly, and steam the vegetables over low heat for 5 minutes.

In a bowl, beat together the egg yolk, lemon juice, nutmeg, salt, and pepper. Place the bowl over a pot of lightly boiling water and stir the ingredients.

Gradually add the hot stock, stirring constantly, until you have a fairly thick sauce. Set the bowl aside.

Wash, dry, and chop the parsley and add to the sauce. Season the sauce and pour over the cauliflower and broccoli. Sprinkle with the sliced almonds and serve immediately.

Serves 2:

1 tbs sliced almonds

9 oz cauliflower

7 oz broccoli

1/2 cup vegetable stock

1 egg yolk

1-2 tsp fresh lemon juice

Freshly ground nutmeg

Salt to taste

Black pepper to taste

1 sprig fresh Italian parsley

Vegetable stock

You can easily make your own fresh stock using onions, mushrooms, carrots, celery, tomatoes, seasonings and herbs.

Sauté chopped onions and mushrooms until they turn dark. Chop the other vegetables and bring to a boil in about 1 quart of water with the seasonings of your choice. Simmer for one hour and let cool. Strain.

power

PER PORTION: 189 calories • 11 g protein • 10 g fat • 17 g carbohydrates

Zucchini and
with stuffed zucchini blossoms
Tomato Salad

Preheat the oven to 350°F. Shake the zucchini blossoms, then gently pull out the pistils from the centers. Peel and finely chop 1 shallot. Peel and grate the carrot. Heat the oil in a small nonstick skillet and gently sauté the chopped shallot and

2 zucchini blossoms (with baby zucchini attached)
3 small shallots
1 small carrot
1 tsp olive oil
3 oz ricotta cheese
Salt to taste
Black pepper to taste
1/2 tsp mustard
1 tbs white wine vinegar
2-3 tbs extra virgin olive oil
5 oz baby zucchini
3 small, firm tomatoes

grated carrot over low heat for a few minutes. In a bowl, mix together the ricotta, sautéed carrot, and shallot, salt, and pepper. Using a teaspoon, carefully fill the zucchini blossoms with the ricotta mixture and fold the petals over the filling. Place the stuffed blossoms in a baking dish and bake in the center of the oven for about 10 minutes, turning once halfway through.

Meanwhile, to make the dressing, peel and chop the remaining 2 shallots and mix with some salt and pepper, the mustard, and vinegar; then beat in the oil.

Wash and trim the zucchini. Wash the tomatoes and remove the stalks. Cut the tomatoes and zucchini into thin slices and arrange on two plates. Pour over the dressing, place the stuffed zucchini blossoms on top, and serve.

PER PORTION: 225 calories • 7 g protein • 18 g fat • 9 g carbohydrates

Vegetable and
with cider vinegar dressing
Herb Salad

In a salad bowl, combine the cider vinegar, salt, and pepper; then, add both oils and beat thoroughly. Season well.

Serves 2:
2 tbs cider vinegar
Salt to taste
White pepper to taste
2 tbs canola oil
1 tbs walnut oil
1 small kohlrabi
10 radishes
3 oz baby carrots
3 oz cucumber
2 green onions
1 tbs walnut halves
1/2 bunch fresh Italian parsley
1/2 bunch fresh basil

Peel the kohlrabi and trim and wash the radishes. Set aside some of the tender kohlrabi and radish leaves. Trim, wash, and peel the carrots. Wash or peel the cucumber. Cut the vegetables into very small dice, or slice thinly.

Trim, wash, and finely slice the green onions. Chop the walnut halves. Wash, shake dry, and chop the reserved vegetable leaves, parsley, and basil.

Carefully stir the vegetables, walnuts, and herbs into the dressing and season the salad again with salt and pepper.

Getting ahead of yourself
You can prepare this salad 1 or 2 hours ahead of time and let it stand. Cover the bowl well with plastic wrap and refrigerate until serving time to avoid vitamin loss.

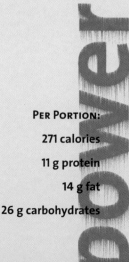

PER PORTION:
271 calories
11 g protein
14 g fat
26 g carbohydrates

Coleslaw with

high in folic acid

Red Onions

Peel and finely chop the onion and combine in a bowl with the vinegars, salt, and pepper. Wash the cress, thyme, and marjoram. Chop the cress and strip the stalks of the thyme and the marjoram. Add the herb leaves to the vinegar mixture, then add the two oils, and beat well.

Trim, wash, and coarsely grate the cabbage. Either use it raw, or blanch in a little salted boiling water for 3-4 minutes. Drain well, then add it to the bowl. Toss well and let stand for about 30 minutes.

Wash and dry the pear. Cut it into quarters and remove the core. Slice the quarters widthwise and toss it in the lemon juice. Arrange on the coleslaw and serve.

Serves 2:
1 red onion
1 tbs cider vinegar
1 tbs white wine vinegar
Salt to taste
Black pepper to taste
1/2 bunch peppercress
1-2 sprigs fresh thyme
1-2 sprigs fresh marjoram
2 tbs sunflower oil
1 tbs pumpkin seed oil
10 oz green cabbage
1 pear
1 tbs fresh lemon juice

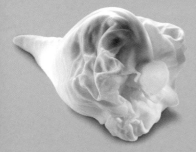

Green cabbage

Green cabbage is a good source of folic acid, which is beneficial just before and during the early stages of pregnancy. Cabbage also contains other B vitamins and carotene. Eat it raw for maximum nutritional benefit.

PER PORTION:

246 calories

4 g protein

13 g fat

30 g carbohydrates

power

Asparagus
Salad
with piquant tomato vinaigrette

Wash the tomato and remove the stalk. Cut it into eighths, remove the seeds, and finely dice. Wash the chives briefly, dry thoroughly, and chop thinly.

In a bowl, mix the apple syrup or honey with the cider vinegar, salt, and pepper. Add the two oils and beat thoroughly. Add the tomato and chives and stir carefully.

Wash and trim the asparagus and peel the lower third. Cut it diagonally into very thin slices and immediately toss it in the dressing. Arrange on plates.

Wash and shake dry the basil. Roughly chop the pistachio nuts. Sprinkle the basil leaves and the pistachio nuts over the salad and serve immediately.

Serves 2:

1 firm tomato

1/2 bunch fresh chives

2 tbs apple syrup, or

1 tbs honey

1 tbs cider vinegar

Salt to taste

White pepper to taste

1 1/2 tbs vegetable oil

2 tbs pistachio oil

10 oz green asparagus

Small fresh basil leaves

2 tbs pistachio nuts

Asparagus

This elegant vegetable is very low in calories–only about 54 calories per 10 oz–and very is high in vitamins A, C, B_1, and B_2. The presence of calcium, phosphorous, potassium, and iodine add to the value of this healthy food. Aspartic acid stimulates kidney activity, making asparagus a good diuretic.

PER PORTION:

248 calories

4 g protein

23 g fat

6 g carbohydrates

power

Fruited
with grapefruit and apple syrup
Raw Carrots

Serves 2: 1 grapefruit • 2 tbs pumpkin seed oil • 1 tbs cider vinegar • 2 tbs apple syrup or 1 tbs honey • Salt to taste • Black pepper to taste • 7 oz carrots • 2 tbs pumpkin seeds

Carefully peel the grapefruit and cut it into segments, collecting the juice in a bowl. Combine the juice with the oil, vinegar, and apple syrup or honey, and stir until smooth. Season with salt and pepper. Peel, trim, and coarsely grate the carrots. Mix with the dressing and arrange on plates with the grapefruit segments. Sprinkle with the pumpkin seeds.

PER PORTION: 196 calories • 6 g protein • 14 g fat • 13 g carbohydrates

Beet
winter power source
Salad

Serves 2: 4 small fresh beets • 1/2 bunch fresh Italian parsley • 1 tsp mustard • 2 tbs white wine vinegar • Salt to taste • Black pepper to taste • 3 tbs olive oil • 2 tbs sliced almonds (toasted)

Wash and scrub the beets thoroughly. Place the unpeeled beets in boiling water and cook for about 30 minutes, until tender. Wash, shake dry, and chop the parsley. Mix with the mustard, vinegar, salt, and pepper; then, beat in the oil. Peel the beets, cut into slices, and then into thick strips. Stir them into the dressing and sprinkle with almonds before serving.

PER PORTION: 190 calories • 3 g protein • 16 g fat • 9 g carbohydrates

Brussels Sprout Salad
and spicy horseradish
with Fresh Pears

Wash and trim the Brussels sprouts and cut an X into the base of the stalks with a paring knife.

Bring the stock to a boil in a saucepan. Place the Brussels sprouts in a steamer insert and place in the saucepan. Cover with a tightly fitting lid and steam over low heat for about 5 minutes.

Peel and core the pear and coarsely grate the flesh. Place in a dish, and immediately add the lemon juice, crème fraîche, and a small amount of the vegetable stock. Whip the cream until stiff and gently fold into the dressing. Stir in the horseradish, and season with salt and pepper.

Cut the roast beef into thick strips, arrange on plates with the Brussels sprouts, and pour the dressing over the top.

Serves 2:
8 oz baby Brussels sprouts
1/2 cup vegetable stock
1 small pear
1 tbs fresh lemon juice
2 tbs crème fraîche
3 tbs heavy cream
2 tsp grated fresh horseradish
Salt to taste
Black pepper to taste
2 oz roast beef, thinly sliced

power

PER PORTION: 252 calories • 11 g protein • 14 g fat • 24 g carbohydrates

Vegetable
with radish vinaigrette
Vitamins

Wash and peel the carrots and horseradish. Wash the zucchini. Grate the carrots, horseradish, and zucchini coarsely, or cut into thin slices. Wash the tomato, remove the stalk, and cut into slices. Wash, trim, and thinly slice the green onion.

Serves 2:
4 oz carrots
1 small piece fresh
horseradish root
1 small zucchini
1 tomato
1 green onion
6 radishes
1 tbs lemon juice
2 tsp apple syrup, or
1 tsp honey
2 tbs cider vinegar
2 tbs sunflower oil
2 tbs olive oil
Salt to taste
Black pepper to taste
1 tbs sunflower kernels

Wash and trim the radishes and leaves. Chop a small amount of the tender radish leaves and set aside. Slice half of the radishes, and coarsely grate the rest.

Combine the chopped radish leaves with the lemon juice, apple syrup or honey, and cider vinegar in a bowl. Beat in the two oils. Stir in the grated radishes, then season the dressing with salt and pepper.

Arrange the remaining ingredients on a serving dish or two individual plates. Pour the radish vinaigrette over the salad and sprinkle with the sunflower kernels.

Radishes and horseradish

These "cousins" contain a generous amount of vitamin C, as well as several other essential vitamins and minerals. Because they are usually eaten raw, you get the maximum benefit from the nutrients.

PER PORTION:
300 calories
9 g protein
19 g fat
23 g carbohydrates

power

Light
the classic Italian soup
Minestrone

Wash, peel, and dice the potatoes. Wash, trim, and chop the leek, zucchini, carrots, and fennel.

Wash the tomato and carefully cut an X into the round end. Place in boiling water for a few moments, then peel and chop roughly, discarding the core. Peel and finely chop the onion.

In a saucepan, heat the oil over medium-low heat and sauté the chopped onion until translucent. Add the fennel, carrots, leek, and zucchini, and sauté gently. Add the stock. Add the tomato and the potatoes. Cover the pan tightly and cook over medium heat for about 20 minutes.

Wash and shake dry the herbs. Remove the leaves from the coarse stalks and chop. Add the herbs to the soup and season with salt and pepper.

Sprinkle with the grated cheese before serving.

Serves 2:
6 oz boiling potatoes
1 baby leek
4 oz zucchini
4 oz carrots
1/2 bulb fennel
1 large tomato
1 small onion
1 tbs olive oil
2 cups hot stock
1/2 bunch fresh Italian parsley
1/2 bunch fresh basil
Salt to taste
Black pepper to taste
1 oz Romano cheese, freshly grated

PER PORTION: 394 calories • 17 g protein • 13 g fat • 54 g carbohydrates

Chilled Spanish
refreshing and full of vitamins
Vegetable Soup

Carefully cut an X into the round ends of the tomatoes. Place in boiling water for a few moments, then peel and chop, discarding the core.

Peel the onion and the cucumber. Halve, trim, and wash the pepper. Finely dice the vegetables. Peel the garlic and place in a blender with the tomatoes and a generous half of the other vegetables. Puree until smooth.

Sprinkle the vinegar and about 1/2 cup water over the bread and let stand for a few minutes. Add to the pureed vegetables with the oil, and puree until smooth. Season with salt and pepper and cover with plastic wrap. Place in the refrigerator to chill for about 30 minutes. Cover the remaining vegetables and place in the refrigerator to chill.

Stir the soup and season. Stir in the remaining vegetables and serve immediately.

Serves 2:
10 oz ripe tomatoes
1 small Spanish onion
1/2 cucumber
1 small green bell pepper
2 cloves garlic
1/2-1 tbs red wine vinegar
1 slice white bread
2 tbs extra virgin olive oil
Salt to taste
Black pepper to taste

Refreshing sources of vitamins

Cold soups are invigorating on hot summer days, and provide generous amounts of vitamins. The vegetables are processed raw, so that most of the vitamins are retained. It is important to cover and chill the soup to let the flavors develop fully.

PER PORTION:
187 calories
5 g protein
9 g fat
23 g carbohydrates

power

Indonesian

with celery and bean sprouts

Vegetable Soup

Pour a generous amount of hot water over the noodles in a bowl and let stand until softened.

Bring 2 cups water to a boil. Wash the chicken and place in the water. Wash the lemon under hot water and remove the zest. Peel and finely chop the ginger. Place both in the water with the chicken, bay leaf, and peanuts. Cover and simmer over low heat for about 30 minutes.

Rinse the bean sprouts under cold water and shake dry. Wash and trim the celery and the green onions. Wash and peel the carrot. Cut the vegetables into thin slices.

Remove the chicken from the stock. Discard the skin and bones and cut the meat into thin slices. Strain the stock and heat through again. Season to taste with soy sauce, pepper, and the juice from the zested lemon. Place the chicken, drained noodles, and sliced vegetables in the stock and cook for 3-4 minutes. Sprinkle with the cilantro leaves and serve.

Serves 2:
- 3/4 oz cellophane noodles
- 4-5 chicken legs
- 1 small lemon
- 1/2 oz fresh ginger
- 1 bay leaf
- 1 tbs roasted peanuts
- 3 oz bean sprouts
- 2 stalks celery
- 2 green onions
- 1 carrot
- 2-3 tbs light soy sauce
- White pepper to taste
- Handful of fresh cilantro leaves

power

PER PORTION: 567 calories • 53 g protein • 30 g fat • 23 g carbohydrates

Cream of
full of vitamin C and fiber
Radish Soup

Thoroughly wash the radishes and leaves. Set some of the tender leaves and 2-3 radishes aside. Roughly chop the remaining radish leaves and the remaining radishes.

Peel and finely dice the shallot. Wash, peel, and roughly chop the potatoes.

Heat the oil in a saucepan over medium heat, add the shallot, and sauté until translucent. Add the chopped radishes, chopped radish leaves, and potatoes and sauté briefly. Pour in the stock. Cover the pan tightly and simmer gently over medium heat for about 20 minutes.

Serves 2:
1 large bunch radishes
1 shallot
4 oz potatoes
2 tbs sunflower oil
1 1/4 cups vegetable stock
2 tbs crème fraîche
Salt to taste
White pepper to taste

Puree the soup in a blender until smooth. Return the soup to the saucepan and heat through. Stir in 1 tbs of the crème fraîche and season with salt and pepper.

Thinly slice the reserved radishes and radish leaves.

Pour the soup into two bowls and spoon the remaining crème fraîche into the centers. Sprinkle with the radish slices and leaves.

power

PER PORTION: 153 calories• 2 g protein• 9 g fat • 14 g carbohydrates

Rutabaga Stew
with lots of carotene and vitamin C
with Meatballs

In a bowl, mix together the ground beef, egg, bread crumbs, salt, pepper, and cayenne pepper. Shape into small meatballs.

Serves 2:
6 oz lean ground beef
1 egg
2-3 tbs bread crumbs
Salt to taste
Black pepper to taste
Cayenne pepper to taste
14 oz rutabaga
1 leek
2 cups vegetable stock
1-2 tsp vegetable oil
1/2 bunch fresh basil
1/2-1 tsp curry powder
1/2 tsp ground cumin

Trim and peel the rutabaga. Cut into thin slices, then into thin strips. Trim the leek, slice lengthwise, and wash thoroughly. Shake dry and cut into thin slices. In a saucepan, bring the stock to a boil. Place the rutabaga and leek in the stock, cover tightly, and simmer gently over low heat for about 10 minutes. Meanwhile, heat the oil over medium heat in a small nonstick skillet. Brown the meatballs on all sides in the oil, about 10 minutes.

Wash and shake dry the basil, setting aside some of the leaves for garnish. Finely chop the remaining leaves and add to the pan with the vegetables.

Season with the curry, cumin, salt, and pepper. Add the meatballs and garnish with the reserved basil.

Rutabagas
Rutabagas, a cross between turnips and cabbage, contain generous amounts of vitamins and minerals, and are especially high in carotene, niacin, vitamin B_6, and vitamin C.

PER PORTION:
464 calories
35 g protein
17 g fat
44 g carbohydrates

power

Sauerkraut Soup
high in vitamin C
with Chive Cream

Serves 2: 1 small onion • 1 small potato • 1 tbs butter • 5 oz sauerkraut (drained) • 2 cups vegetable stock • Salt to taste • Black pepper to taste • 1 bunch fresh chives • 3 tbs sour cream

Peel and finely dice the onion and potato, and sauté both in the butter in a saucepan until the onion is translucent. Add the sauerkraut and the stock, cover, and simmer gently for about 10 minutes. Puree the mixture and season well. Pour back into the saucepan and heat through. Wash and chop the chives and combine with the sour cream, salt, and pepper. Pour over the soup before serving.

PER PORTION: 253 calories • 7 g protein • 11 g fat • 33 g carbohydrates

Creamy
with toasted almonds
Leek Soup

Serves 2: 1 leek • 4 oz potatoes • 1 cup vegetable stock • Salt to taste • White pepper to taste • 1 tsp fresh thyme leaves • 3 tbs plain yogurt • 2 tbs sliced almonds (toasted)

Cut the leek in half lengthwise, wash, trim, and cut into slices. Peel, wash, and finely chop the potatoes. Place both in a saucepan with the stock, cover tightly, and simmer gently for 15 minutes. Puree the soup and season with salt, pepper, and the thyme. Pour back into the saucepan and heat through. Stir in the yogurt and garnish with the almonds.

PER PORTION: 187 calories • 8 g protein • 7 g fat • 24 g carbohydrates

Curried Ginger
with chile and coconut milk
Vegetables

Slit open the chile, trim, wash, and cut into thin rings. Peel and finely chop the garlic and ginger. Wash, trim, and slice the green onions. Wash and trim the snow peas and cut into thirds diagonally. Wash and peel the carrots. Cut into thin strips lengthwise, then slice as thinly as possible. Rinse the bean sprouts in a sieve and drain well.

Heat the oil in a wok over medium-high heat. Add the garlic, ginger, and chile rings and stir-fry lightly. Add the snow peas and carrots and stir-fry for 2-3 minutes. Then, add the green onions and stir-fry for a minute or two. Add the coconut milk, curry paste, and soy sauce and heat through. Add the bean sprouts and heat for another 1-2 minutes. Wash and roughly chop a few cilantro leaves. Sprinkle over the vegetables and serve immediately.

Serves 2:

1 red chile
1 clove garlic
Thumb-sized piece fresh ginger
1/2 bunch green onions
4 oz snow peas
5 oz carrots
3 oz fresh bean sprouts
1 tbs vegetable oil
1 cup unsweetened coconut milk
1-2 tsp hot curry paste
3 tbs light soy sauce
Fresh cilantro leaves

power

PER PORTION: 234 calories • 6 g protein • 16 g fat • 19 g carbohydrates

Stir-Fried Squash

with curry, chiles, and grapes

with Brown Rice

In a saucepan, gently heat 1/2 tbs of the olive oil over medium heat. Stir in the rice, then pour in the stock and cover tightly. Cook over low heat until just firm to the bite (20-40 minutes, depending on the type of rice; refer to the instructions on the package).

Serves 2:
2 tbs extra virgin olive oil
1/2 cup brown rice
1 cup vegetable stock
About 1 lb butternut squash
Salt to taste
1/2 bunch green onions
1-2 small red chiles
1 small clove garlic
2 oz seedless green grapes
1/4-1/2 tbs curry powder
Black pepper to taste
2-3 tbs pumpkin seeds

Peel the squash and remove the seeds and tough fibers. Cut the squash flesh into 1/2-3/4-inch pieces. Bring 1/2 cup of lightly salted water to a boil in a saucepan. Place the squash in the boiling water, cover tightly and cook for about 5 minutes. Drain, reserving the cooking liquid.

Wash and trim the green onions and cut them diagonally into thin rings. Trim the chiles, remove the seeds, rinse, and finely chop. Peel and finely chop the garlic. Rinse the grapes under hot water.

Heat the remaining 1 tbs oil in a wok or large skillet over medium-high heat. Add the chopped chile and garlic and stir-fry gently for about 2 minutes. Stir in the curry powder and the reserved squash cooking liquid. Add the grapes and the squash flesh to the pan. Season with salt and pepper and cover. Cook over low heat for another 5 minutes.

Drain the rice. Combine all the ingredients, season, and sprinkle with the pumpkin seeds before serving.

power

PER PORTION: 519 calories • 18 g protein • 19 g fat • 74 g carbohydrates

Spanish Potato
with zucchini, red pepper, and leek
Tortilla

Wash the potatoes and cook unpeeled in a small amount of salted water with the cumin for about 20 minutes, until tender. Drain, cool slightly, and peel. Cut into thick slices.

Wash the zucchini, cut it in half lengthwise, and slice. Halve, trim, and wash the pepper, and chop. Trim the leek, slit it lengthwise, and wash it well. Shake it dry and cut into thin rings.

Heat the oil in a large nonstick skillet over medium-high heat. Sauté the potatoes in the oil until golden brown. Add the sliced zucchini, chopped pepper, and sliced leek, and cook over low heat for about 5 minutes, stirring gently.

Serves 2:
8 oz boiling potatoes
Salt to taste
1 tbs ground cumin
1 small zucchini
1 red bell pepper
1 small leek
2 tbs olive oil
1 red chile
1 small clove garlic
4 eggs
Black pepper to taste

Slit open the chile, remove the seeds, and finely chop the flesh. Peel and chop the garlic. Beat the chile and garlic with the eggs and season with salt and pepper. Pour the egg mixture over the potatoes and vegetables. Cover with a lid and place over very low heat for about 5 minutes, until the eggs are set. Invert onto a cutting board and cut into wedges to serve.

power

PER PORTION: 474 calories • 31 gprotein • 30 g fat • 20 g carbohydrates

Provençal
a light classic from the south of France
Peppers

Soak a small clay pot and lid in water for 15-30 minutes. Meanwhile, halve, seed, and core the peppers. Wash the pepper halves and cut them into strips.

Serves 2:
1 each small red, yellow, and green bell pepper
1 lb beefsteak tomatoes
4 oz zucchini
1 medium onion
1 clove garlic
2 sprigs fresh rosemary
3-4 sprigs fresh thyme
Salt to taste
Black pepper to taste
2 tsp fresh lemon juice
1 tbs olive oil
1/2 cup vegetable stock

Cut an X into the round ends of the tomatoes and place in boiling water for a few moments. Remove them with a slotted spoon, then peel, remove the core, and chop roughly. Wash, trim, and roughly chop the zucchini. Peel and finely chop the onion and garlic. Wash and shake dry the herbs, setting some aside for garnish. Finely chop the rest.

Place the vegetables in the clay pot with the salt, pepper, lemon juice, oil, and stock. Cover with the lid and place in the bottom of a cold oven. Turn on the oven heat to 400°F and bake for about 1 hour. Stir the vegetables, season, and sprinkle with the reserved herbs before serving.

✳ Gentle cooking in a clay pot

Cooking in a clay pot is the perfect way to cook vegetables and retain the maximum amount of vitamins, although they take somewhat longer than when cooked in a saucepan. In clay-pot cooking, the vegetables steam gently in their own juices in a firmly sealed container. A minimum of fat is used, and the vegetables turn out wonderfully light and aromatic.

PER PORTION:
175 calories
6 g protein
6 g fat
24 g carbohydrates

power

Salsify and

with plenty of vitamins B₁ and E

Ham Ragout

Thoroughly wash the salsify. Bring a large, wide pot of water to a boil and add the salt and vinegar. Boil the salsify for about 15-20 minutes, taking care not to let it become too soft.

Serves 2:
About 1 lb salsify
Salt to taste
2 tbs white vinegar
1 small onion
1 tbs butter
2 tbs flour
1/2 cup vegetable stock
1/2 cup milk
White pepper to taste
4 oz smoked ham (about 1 thick slice)
1/2 bunch fresh basil

Drain the salsify and rinse under cold water. Either pull off or peel the dark skin (wear rubber gloves), then cut the salsify into 1$\frac{1}{4}$-1$\frac{1}{2}$-inch lengths.

Peel and finely chop the onion. Melt the butter in a saucepan over medium heat and sauté the onion until translucent. Sprinkle the flour over the onion and cook, stirring constantly, until golden. Gradually add the stock and the milk. Cook, stirring, until slightly thickened, then season well with salt and pepper. Dice the ham. Wash and finely chop the basil. Add both to the pot with the salsify and heat through. Season well.

Salsify

Salsify is easy to digest and contains good amounts of vitamins, such as A (carotene), B₁, and E. Diabetics will be interested to learn of its high insulin level–a carbohydrate that poses no problem.

PER PORTION:

274 calories

15 g protein

11 g fat

16 g carbohydrates

power

Stovetop Spelt Cakes

healthy and elegant

with Radishes

Gently toast the spelt in a small dry saucepan over medium heat. Pour in the stock and bring to a simmer. Cover with a lid and simmer for about 10 minutes over low heat, then remove from the heat and let stand until plumped, about 20 minutes.

Wash and trim the radishes and leaves. Finely chop a few of the tender leaves. Cut the radishes into four or eight pieces each. Peel and finely chop the onion.

Melt 1 tbs of the butter in a skillet over medium heat and gently sauté the onion until translucent. Add the radishes and tops. Season well with salt and pepper, then cover and cook over low heat for about 5 minutes. Do not add any more liquid.

Serves 2:

3 oz ground spelt

1/2 cup vegetable stock

1 large bunch radishes

1 red onion

2 tbs butter

Salt to taste

Black pepper to taste

2 eggs

1 tbs crème fraîche

Beat the eggs and stir them into the spelt. Season with salt and pepper. Melt the remaining 1 tbs butter in a nonstick skillet over medium heat. Drop small amounts of the spelt mixture into the pan and sauté until golden brown on both sides. Check the flavor of the radish mixture, then arrange on plates on top of the spelt cakes. Add a tiny dollop of crème fraîche to each plate and serve immediately.

power

PER PORTION: 390 calories • 20 g protein • 18 g fat • 37 g carbohydrates

Carrot Crêpes
with herbed cottage cheese
with Asparagus

To make the crêpes, mix the eggs, salt, water, and flour. Cover and let stand for about 30 minutes.

Wash, trim, and peel the asparagus. Bring a small amount of water to a boil in a saucepan with some salt, 2 tbs of butter, and the sugar. Place the asparagus in a steamer insert and lower it into the saucepan. Cover tightly and steam over low heat for 5-8 minutes, until tender-crisp.

Beat together the cottage cheese, apple syrup or honey, lemon juice, salt, and pepper. Thin the mixture slightly with a little milk. Wash the herbs, shake dry, and chop; add to the cottage cheese mixture. Season well with salt and pepper.

Wash, trim, and peel the carrots. Grate them finely and add to the crêpe batter. In a nonstick skillet, cook two crêpes in succession, melting about 1 tsp butter in the pan for each one; cook until golden brown on both sides. Drain the asparagus, divide into two equal portions, and wrap a crêpe around each portion. Place on plates and serve with the herbed cottage cheese.

Serves 2:
2 eggs
Salt to taste
1/2 cup water
1/3 cup flour
1 3/4 lb white or green asparagus
1/4 cup butter
1 tsp sugar
4 oz low-fat cottage cheese
1/2 tbs apple syrup, or
3/4 tsp honey
1/2 tbs fresh lemon juice
Black pepper to taste
Milk
1/2 bunch mixed fresh herbs
3 oz carrots

power

PER PORTION: 415 calories • 25 g protein • 17 g fat • 30 g carbohydrates

Turnip and Turkey
great with brown rice
Fricassee

Wash, trim, and slice the turnips and the carrots, halving any large slices. Place the slices in a steamer insert.

Bring a small amount of salted water to a boil in a small saucepan. Place the steamer insert with the vegetables in the saucepan, cover tightly, and steam the vegetables over low heat for about 10 minutes, until still slightly firm to the bite.

Serves 2:
7 oz small white turnips
7 oz carrots
Salt to taste
7 oz turkey breast
1/2 bunch fresh basil
1 tbs butter
2 tbs flour
1/2 cup milk
1/2 cup chicken stock
Black pepper to taste
Fresh lemon juice to taste
1-2 tbs dried mushroom powder

Meanwhile, rinse the turkey under cold water, pat dry with paper towels, and cut into small pieces. Wash and shake dry the basil, putting some of the leaves aside as garnish, and finely chop the rest.

Melt the butter in a wide saucepan, add the turkey and sauté until golden brown on all sides. Sprinkle the flour over the turkey, stir to combine, then gradually add the milk and stock. Simmer the sauce gently for 5 minutes over low heat, stirring occasionally, until thickened.

Add the prepared vegetables and the chopped basil and return the mixture to a boil. Season the fricassee with salt, pepper, lemon juice, and the dried mushrooms. Garnish with the basil leaves before serving.

PER PORTION: 310 calories • 29 g protein • 6 g fat• 21 g carbohydrates

Stir-Fried
with hot chile and sweet pineapple
Thai Vegetables

Peel and finely chop the garlic and ginger. Slit open the chile and scrape out the seeds. Rinse the chile and slice into thin rings. Wash and trim the broccoli and divide into florets. Peel and chop the broccoli stalks. Wash and peel the carrot and cut diagonally into thin slices. Wash and pick over the bok choy or cabbage, and cut into thick slices. Wash and trim the green onions and cut diagonally into thin slices. Peel the pineapple, remove the core, and cut into small dice.

Heat the oil in a wok or large skillet over medium-high heat. Add the garlic, ginger, and chile rings and stir-fry briefly. Add the broccoli and carrot and stir-fry for about 2 minutes. Add the green onions and stir-fry for 1 minute. Sprinkle the sugar over the vegetables and pour in the stock. Add the bok choy, pineapple, fish sauce, and a squeeze of lime juice and bring to a boil. Serve garnished with cilantro leaves.

Serves 2:
1 clove garlic
Thumb-sized piece fresh ginger
1 red chile
8 oz broccoli
1 carrot
3 oz baby bok choy or
Chinese cabbage
2 green onions
2-3 slices fresh pineapple
1 tbs vegetable oil
2 tsp brown sugar
1/2 cup vegetable stock
2 tbs Thai fish sauce (*nam pla*)
Lime juice to taste
Fresh cilantro leaves

power

PER PORTION: 235 calories • 8 g protein • 10 g fat • 33 g carbohydrates

Linguine with Raw
aromatic and low in calories
Tomato Sauce

Cut an X into the round ends of the tomatoes and place in boiling water for a few moments. Remove from the water, peel, and remove the core and seeds. Chop into small pieces.

Serves 2:
1 lb ripe tomatoes
1 clove garlic
2 tbs fruity extra virgin olive oil
Salt to taste
Black pepper to taste
8 oz linguine
Fresh basil
2 tbs freshly grated Parmesan cheese

Peel and finely chop the garlic. Place in a bowl with the tomatoes and oil, and season with salt and pepper. Cover and set aside.

Cook the linguine in a large amount of boiling salted water until slightly firm to the bite (*al dente*). Drain well in a sieve.

Stir the tomato sauce and taste. Heat through briefly, then combine with the pasta and serve immediately. Wash and dry the basil and sprinkle over the pasta to taste, along with the Parmesan.

Tomatoes

Most pasta sauces are cooked for long periods of time, which reduces their vitamin content. In this briefly cooked sauce, the tomatoes are still bursting with A, C, E, and B complex vitamins when you sit down to eat. Tomatoes are also low in calories, diuretic, and good for the blood.

PER PORTION:

512 calories

18 g protein

12 g fat

81 g carbohydrates

power

Mixed Fresh
with refreshing yogurt cream
Berries

Mix the yogurt with the apple syrup or honey, milk, and a small amount of ground cinnamon, and divide among two dessert plates.

Wash the lemon thoroughly under hot running water and dry well. Finely grate the lemon zest and squeeze the juice. Mix both in a bowl with the sugar. Wash, pick over, and drain the berries and grapes or currants. Wash the plums and remove the stones. Cut the plums into segments. Carefully stir the plum segments into the lemon juice mixture.

Arrange all of the fruit on top of the yogurt, sprinkle lightly with cinnamon, and serve immediately.

Serves 2:

4 oz low-fat plain yogurt

1 tbs apple syrup, or

1/2 tbs honey

2 tbs milk

1/2 tsp ground cinnamon, plus more for garnish

1/2 lemon

1 tbs sugar, or more to taste

2 oz small fresh raspberries

2 oz fresh blackberries

2 oz fresh blueberries

2 oz small seedless red grapes or red currants

2 fresh yellow plums

PER PORTION: 173 calories • 4 g protein• 1 g fat • 38 g carbohydrates power

Strawberry and
contains plenty of vitamin C
Kiwi Salad

Serves 2: 1/2 lime • 1 tbs maple syrup • Pinch of vanilla powder • 8 oz small fresh strawberries • 2 kiwis • 1-2 tbs pecans (roughly chopped)

Wash the lime under hot running water, grate the zest, and squeeze the juice. Combine the zest and juice with the maple syrup and vanilla. Wash the strawberries briefly, remove the stalks, and cut thickly. Peel and halve the kiwis and cut into slices. Arrange the fruit on plates, pour over the syrup, and top with the pecans.

PER PORTION: 104 calories • 1 g protein • 5 g fat • 15 g carbohydrates

Date and
with lime juice and honey
Pineapple Salad

Serves 2: 1/2 small fresh pineapple • 1 kiwi • 4 fresh dates • 2 tbs fresh lime juice • 2 tsp brown sugar • 1 tbs floral honey • 1 tbs dried coconut (toasted)

Peel the pineapple, cut lengthwise into fourths, and remove the core. Cut into slices, saving as much of the juice as possible. Peel and halve the kiwi and slice the halves. Remove the pits from the dates and cut into segments. Stir together the lime and pineapple juices, sugar, and honey. Mix the juice mixture with the fruit and sprinkle with the toasted coconut.

PER PORTION: 125 calories • 1 g protein • 1 g fat • 31 g carbohydrates

Melon and Mango
refreshing and healthy
Soup with Kiwi

Halve the orange and squeeze the juice. Halve the melon and remove the seeds and fibers. Using a melon baller, scoop several small balls out of the melon flesh; cover and place in the refrigerator. Remove the rest of the melon flesh from the skin. Peel the mango and cut the flesh from the pit. Puree the melon and mango flesh with the orange juice, and strain through a sieve. Flavor the soup with lemon juice and a few drops of bitters, and divide among two chilled bowls.

Halve and peel the kiwi and cut into slices. Place in the soup, together with the melon balls. Garnish with a few lemon balm or mint leaves.

Serves 2:
1 orange, well chilled
1/2 ripe melon, such as cantaloupe, well chilled
1 small ripe mango, well chilled
1-2 tbs fresh lemon juice
Angostura bitters
1 kiwi
Fresh lemon balm or mint leaves

Melons, mangos, and kiwis

All these fruits are very low in calories and very high in vitamins and other "goodies." Melons are diuretic and generally cleansing, so they are an ideal part of any diet or beauty regime. Mangos provide carotene and B complex vitamins; kiwis contain generous amounts of vitamin C.

PER PORTION:
122 calories
2 g protein
1 g fat
31 g carbohydrates

Jellied
with juicy plums
Buttermilk Soup

Pour the buttermilk into a small saucepan and sprinkle with 1 package of gelatin. Let stand for 5 minutes, then heat gently, stirring, to dissolve the gelatin. Cool. Repeat the soaking and dissolving procedure with the apple juice and remaining gelatin.

1 1/2 packages unflavored gelatin
1 cup buttermilk
1/2 cup apple juice
1/2 tsp grated lemon zest
2 tbs apple syrup, or
1 tbs honey
1/2 tsp ground cinnamon
5 oz fresh plums

Mix the buttermilk mixture with the lemon zest, apple syrup or honey, and ground cinnamon. Pour into 2 small soup plates and chill until set. Do not chill the apple juice.

Wash and halve the plums and remove the stones. Arrange the plums on the jellied buttermilk, cut into fan shapes, if desired. Pour over the apple juice and place in the refrigerator to set, covering the plates with plastic wrap to prevent vitamin loss.

Plums

Carotene, B vitamins, and vitamin C are prominent in these fruits, which also contain plenty of minerals. The optimum benefit is gained from the plums' carotene, the precursor to vitamin A, if you slice open the fruit and combine them with a little fat (as in the buttermilk). This recipe is also delicious made with strawberries.

PER PORTION:

207 calories

7 g protein

1 g fat

47 g carbohydrates

power

Citrus Fruit
with creamed cottage cheese
Platter

Wash the lime and lemon in hot water and dry well. Remove some of the zest in fine strips, and finely grate some of the rest. Squeeze the juice of both fruits. Combine the juice and the grated zest with the maple syrup and cottage cheese and mix well.

Peel the orange and the grapefruit, removing all of the bitter white pith. Remove the fruit segments from between the membranes.

Divide the cottage cheese mixture among two plates. Arrange the orange and grapefruit segments decoratively on top. Roughly chop the pecans and sprinkle over the desserts with the chocolate flakes and grated lime and lemon zests.

Serves 2:
1 small lime
1/2 lemon
2 tbs maple syrup
4 oz low-fat cottage cheese
1 large orange
1 large pink grapefruit
1 oz pecans
2 tsp shaved chocolate

Citrus fruits

Whether grapefruit, lime, orange, or lemon, citrus fruits provide lots of beta carotene and vitamin C, and contain large quantities of minerals. Because the vitamins are delicate, you should always eat citrus fruit as soon as you have peeled it. Almost as good: drink a large glass of freshly squeezed juice.

PER PORTION:

332 calories

15 g protein

18 g fat

37 g carbohydrates

Jellied Fruit Tea
a little light relief
with Grapes

Brew the fruit tea in a teapot with the boiling water and steep for 5 minutes. Soak the gelatin in the cold water for 5 minutes.

Wash the lemon in hot water and dry. Finely grate the zest and squeeze the juice. Dissolve the gelatin in the hot tea. Add the lemon juice and zest and 1 tbs of the sugar.

Wash the grapes and set some aside for garnish; halve the remaining grapes and remove the seeds, if necessary. Divide the grapes among two tall glasses and pour over the tea. Cover and refrigerate until set.

Beat the yogurt with the remaining 1 tbs sugar. Pour onto the jellied tea and serve garnished with grapes.

Serves 2:

3 tbs fruit tea leaves

1 cup water

1 package unflavored gelatin

1/2 cup cold water

1/2 lemon

2 tbs confectioners' sugar

3 oz each red and green grapes

3 oz low-fat plain yogurt

Grapes

Grapes are full of glucose, which provides instant energy when consumed. Although the amount of vitamins does not quite compare with the levels in other fruits, grapes are nevertheless valuable. They stimulate the metabolism and the digestive system, detoxify the body, stimulate the reproduction of blood cells, and are generally beneficial to health, looks, and well-being.

PER PORTION:

101 calories

4 g protein

1 g fat

22 g carbohydrates

power

Blueberry and

full of vitamin B$_6$ and folic acid

Banana Milk

Briefly wash, then pick over the blueberries, and drain well. Peel and roughly chop the banana and sprinkle with the lemon juice. Puree the blueberries with the banana and the pear syrup or honey in a blender. Stir in the vanilla and cold milk. Pour into glasses and serve immediately.

Serves 2:

8 oz blueberries

1 small ripe banana

1 tbs fresh lemon juice

1 tbs pear syrup, or

1/2 tbs honey

Dash of vanilla extract

1 1/4 cups ice-cold milk

Blueberries and bananas

Blueberries contain large amounts of the protective substances carotene and vitamin C—reason enough to treat yourself to them as often as you like. Other plus points: the blue coloring and tannic acids present in the skin both aid in blood reproduction and are cleansing.

Although bananas contain more energy-producing qualities than other fruits, they also contain certain vitamins that other fruits do not, especially pantothenic acid and folic acid, which are rarely found in fruits.

PER PORTION:

265 calories

10 g protein

10 g fat

35 g carbohydrates

Raspberry and
berry, berry healthy
Strawberry Shake

Wash and pick over the berries. Use a sharp knife to hull the strawberries.

Puree the berries in a blender and strain through a fine sieve to remove

the seeds.

Add the pear syrup or honey, cinnamon, and vanilla

to the fruit puree. Add the cottage cheese and milk,

pulsing briefly to combine.

Pour the shake into glasses and serve immediately.

Serves 2:
3 oz raspberries
3 oz strawberries
2 tbs pear syrup, or 1 tbs honey
Pinch of ground cinnamon
Dash of vanilla extract
1/2 cup low-fat cottage cheese
1/2 cup milk

Raspberries and strawberries

Just 4 oz of strawberries will give you your
daily requirement of vitamin C, the most
important vitamin for disease resistance. Its
other components make this delicious fruit a
popular choice for health and beauty.
Strawberries quickly lose their flavor and
vitamins, so eat them as soon as possible after
picking. Raspberries are almost equally
healthy (and sensitive), but do not contain
quite the same levels of vitamins.

PER DRINK:

216 calories

15 g protein

8 g fat

22 g carbohydrates

Fruity
best served well chilled
Cucumber Drink

Serves 2: 7 oz cucumber (well chilled) • 2 kiwis (well chilled) • 1/2 tsp ground ginger • Salt to taste • Black pepper to taste • Well-chilled mineral water

Peel and roughly chop the cucumber, then puree in a blender. Peel and roughly chop the kiwis. Add to the pureed cucumber and blend again briefly. Do not process for long, as otherwise the shake will become bitter. Add the ground ginger, salt, and pepper, and pour into tall glasses. Top with well-chilled mineral water and serve immediately.

PER DRINK: 42 calories • 1 g protein • 1 g fat • 10 g carbohydrates

Carrot and
a healthy snack
Tomato Yogurt

Serves 2: 1/2 cup low-fat yogurt • 1 cup tomato juice • 1/2 cup carrot juice • Salt to taste • Black pepper to taste • Pinch of ground cumin • Lime juice to taste • 2 slices of lime

Combine the yogurt with the tomato and carrot juices in a blender and blend for a few seconds. Flavor the drink with salt, pepper, cumin, and a dash of lime juice and pour into glasses. Serve garnished with lime slices.

PER DRINK: 143 calories • 4 g protein • 1 g fat • 10 g carbohydrates

Iced Pineapple and
an exotic burst of vitamins
Almond Shake

Peel the pineapple, removing the brown "eyes." Cut the fruit into fourths lengthwise and remove the hard core from the segments. Roughly chop the fruit and place in a blender.

Serves 2:
1/2 small ripe pineapple
1/2 lime
1 tbs brown sugar
1 tbs unsweetened almond butter
4 oz vanilla frozen yogurt
Crushed ice
1 small kiwi
Fresh mint

Squeeze the juice from the lime and add to the blender with the sugar and almond butter. Puree until smooth. Add the frozen yogurt and blend again briefly, until smooth.

Fill 2 tall glasses with crushed ice and pour in the shake. Cut the kiwi (peeled or unpeeled) into segments or thick slices. Garnish the shakes with the kiwi slices and mint leaves.

Pineapple

This tropical fruit has high levels of vitamins A, B, and C. The flesh contains *bromelin*, an enzyme that separates protein in the body, and thus stimulates the digestion of protein. Incidentally, this enzyme is also responsible for the incompatibility between fresh pineapple and gelatin–it prevents the gelatin from setting. Pineapple contains only a few calories, is diuretic, and detoxifying; it is a useful part of any diet.

PER DRINK:

167 calories

5 g protein

6 g fat

25 g carbohydrates

power

Index

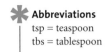

Abbreviations

tsp = teaspoon
tbs = tablespoon

Published originally under the title
VITAMIN DIÄT: Natürlich abnehmen mit
Obst und Gemüse

©1999 Gräfe und Unzer Verlag GmbH,
Munich
English translation copyright for the US
edition: © 2000 Silverback Books, Inc.

Editors: Ina Schröter, Jennifer Newens, CCP
Readers: Dipl. oec. troph. Maryna Zimdars,
Vené Franco
Layout and design: Heinz Kraxenberger
Production: Helmut Giersberg,
Shanti Nelson
Photos: FoodPhotography Eising, Munich
Typeset: Easy Pic Library, Munich
Reproduction: Repro Schmidt, Dornbirn
Printing: Appl, Wemding
Binding: Sellier, Freising

ISBN: 1-930603-15-0

Caution
The techniques and recipes in this book are
to be used at the reader's sole discretion
and risk. Always consult a doctor before
beginning a new eating plan.

Angelika Ilies
Angelika, who was born in Hamburg,
studied ecotrophology and then began her
career in London, where she experienced
working life in a renowned publishing
house. Back in her own country, she added
her support to Germany's leading food
magazine. Since 1989 she has enjoyed a suc-
cessful career as a freelance writer and food
journalist.

Susie M. and **Pete Eising** have studios in
Munich and Kennebunkport, Maine/USA.
They studied at the Munich Academy of
Photography, where they established their
own studio for food photography in 1991.

For this book:
Photographic layout:
Martina Görlach
Food styling:
Monika Schuster

SILVERBACK

BOOKS, INC.

www.silverbackbooks.com